Historic of Ho

The Greater Cots

Gloucestershire, Herefordshire, Oxfordshire
and Warwickshire

Contents

Coughton Court

Connections

The historic houses in this book are scattered across a rich countryside that stretches from the Thames Valley to the Welsh Marches. Diverse as they are, one only has to start delving into their histories to come across some intriguing connections between them.

One such link is provided by the author George Eliot who, as Mary Ann Evans, was born in 1819 at South Farm on the estate of **Arbury Hall** where her father was the steward. In her novel, *Scenes from Clerical Life* she describes one of the rooms in this masterpiece of the late 18th century Gothic Revival as being 'like a cathedral....richly carved pendants, all of creamy white relieved here and there by touches of gold'.

In later life George Eliot became a close friend of Charles, 3rd Earl Somers, the owner of **Eastnor Castle** where the vast Drawing Room, designed by Pugin, is perhaps *the* most spectacular expression of the High Gothic Revival style. Although built in the early 19th century, this memorably romantic castle with its massive Norman proportions recalls the great fortresses established along the Welsh borders during the reign of Edward I.

Citadels such as **Berkeley Castle**, a formidable pile in lovely pink-grey stone that overlooks the river Severn. It was here that the effete King Edward II was gruesomely murdered in 1327. Visitors may still see the room in which he was confined with, nearby, the 28ft deep dungeon into which the rotting carcasses of animals were tossed, to be followed by the living bodies of prisoners.

Three centuries later, during the Civil War, Berkeley was assailed by Parliamentary forces. One of their cannonballs crashed through the Keep, taking a huge bite out of the massive wall. When Cromwell later returned the Castle to the Berkeleys, he imposed a legal stipulation that the breach should never be repaired. It never has been.

Broughton Castle can claim an even more significant rôle in the Civil War, for it was here that the owner, the 7th Baron Saye & Sele, gathered with other leading Puritans such as

Arbury Hall, well-known to George Eliot as a child

Hampden and Pym to plot the downfall of Charles I. Yet only a generation earlier, Charles' father, James I, had stayed at Broughton and honoured his host by making him a viscount. That royal visit took place in 1604, a year when Catholic activists were already hatching the Gunpowder Plot.

The base for *this* conspiracy was the enchanting Elizabethan mansion, **Coughton Court**. It had been rented by Sir Everard Digby whose nephew, Robert Catesby, was the ringleader of the plot. Both were later barbarously executed but Coughton's owner, Thomas Throckmorton, was not implicated. Throughout the next two centuries of persecution, he and his descendants remained faithful to the Old Religion and to this day the Throckmortons remain in possession of both Coughton Court and their Catholic faith.

The Stonors of **Stonor Park** were equally staunch. In 1577, Dame Cecily Stonor her annual fine for recusancy was set at the equivalent of £50,000, a staggering penalty which did not however deter her from giving sanctuary to the Jesuit priest and martyr, Edmund Campion. From a secret room in the roof, he supervised the printing of his defence of Catholicism, *Decem Rationes,* 'Ten Reasons'. When his printing press was discovered at Stonor, the doughty Dame Cecily was thrown into prison from which she emerged to continue helping clandestine priests.

A woman of comparable mettle was Sarah, Duchess of Marlborough. She had wanted **Blenheim Palace** to be a large, comfortable country house but her husband chose as architect Sir John Vanbrugh who envisaged a building on an heroic scale that would challenge the grandeur of Louis XIV's Versailles. The sharp-tongued Sarah constantly harassed Vanbrugh with insults and complaints until he finally left in a fury. When his monumental palace was completed, the Duchess refused him entry even to the Park

No book about historic houses would be complete without an entry for Elizabeth I. On September 9th, 1592, while making a royal progress through Gloucestershire, the Virgin Queen 'dyned at Mr Cotons at Whytington', a charming Tudor mansion known today as **Whittington Court**. From here, the Queen travelled the few miles north to **Sudeley Castle** where Giles, Lord Chandos, laid on three days of extravagant feasting to mark the fourth anniversary of the Spanish Armada's defeat.

The 3rd Marquess of Hertford was no doubt an equally hospitable host when he entertained the Prince Regent at his magnificent Palladian mansion, **Ragley Hall.** The Marquess was rich, charming, intelligent ~ and as diligent in his pursuit of pleasure as 'Prinny' himself. The present Prince of Wales' rather different interest in vernacular architecture led him to **Owlpen Manor,** where he hailed this uniquely beautiful ensemble of Manor House, Church, Mill and cottages of pearl-grey stone as 'the epitome of the English village'.

Like many historic houses, Owlpen has its resident ghosts, the most senior in rank being Henry VI's Queen, Margaret of Anjou, who stayed there in 1471. Even she is outranked by the ghost of Charles I which appears at **Chavenage**. The owner of Chavenage, Col. Nathaniel Stephens, had reluctantly assented to the King's execution. As he lay on his death-bed a hearse, driven by a headless man, drew up at the door of the manor house. The Colonel entered the carriage and the driver as he sped away assumed the shape of the martyr King.

There are no accredited ghosts at **Kelmscott Manor** but a very strong presence ~ that of William Morris, poet, craftsman and socialist who revolutionised English ideas of house decoration and furnishings and for whom this enchanting Elizabethan manor provided the 'the loveliest haunt of ancient peace'.

No ghosts, shades of murdered Kings, or even the turmoil of the Civil War perturb the serenity of **Stanway House.** A dwelling place at peace with itself and the world, its towering oriel windows open upon a scene where for centuries the only changes have been those ordained by the passing of the seasons.

David Gerrard

Berkeley Castle where Edward II was murdered

Map A ~ The Malverns, Evesham and Warwickshire

A458

A442

Stourbridge

A4117

Kidderminster

A456

A448

A443

A449

M5

A448

Redditc

A44

Worcester

A422

5. Ragl

A4103

A449

MALVERN HILLS

Great Malvern

A4104

A44

A417

A4104

A38

VALE

4. Eastnor Castle

Ledbury

A4104

A435

A449

A417

A438

M50

M5

B4077

Tewkesbury

Winchcombe

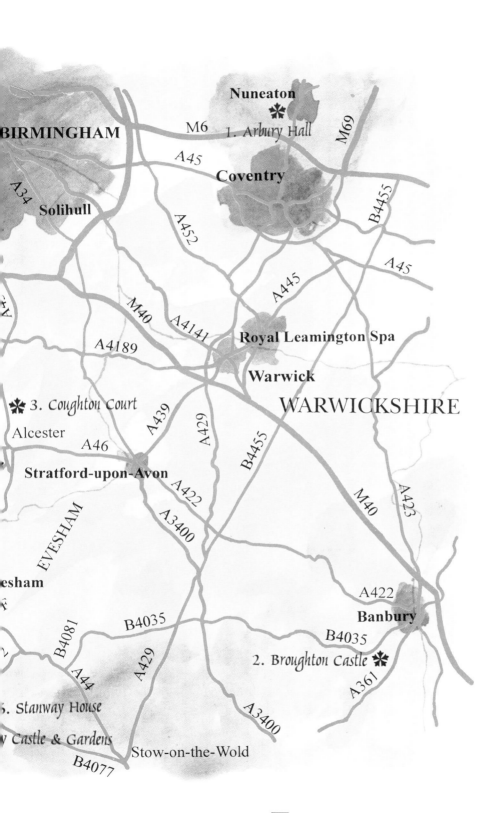

BIRMINGHAM

M6

Nuneaton
❄
1. Arbury Hall

M69

A45

Coventry

A34

Solihull

B4455

A452

A45

A445

M40

A4141

Royal Leamington Spa

A4189

Warwick

WARWICKSHIRE

❄ 3. Coughton Court

A439

A429

Alcester

B4455

A46

Stratford-upon-Avon

A422

EVESHAM

A3400

M40

A423

esham

A422

Banbury

B4081

B4035

B4035

A429

2. Broughton Castle ❄

A44

. Stanway House

A3400

A361

y Castle & Gardens

B4077

Stow-on-the-Wold

Arbury Hall

'Surely the finest Gothic Revival house in the country' ~ Hugh Massingberd

Although the Newdegate family has lived at Arbury for more than 400 years, their tenure began in signally inauspicious circumstances. John Newdegate was a Member of Elizabeth I's Parliament and the owner of a valuable estate in Middlesex but he was also spectacularly incompetent at managing his finances. Matters became so desperate that in 1584 he was declared an outlaw for non-payment of debts.

Two years later, John made an arrangement with Edmund Anderson, Chief Justice of the Common Pleas and owner of Arbury. A spiritual forebear of Judge Jeffreys, Anderson was an irascible jurist, notorious for his 'many oaths and reproachful revilings on the bench'. But the terms he agreed with John Newdegate seem generous enough. In return for his Middlesex estate, John acquired Arbury and Anderson also undertook to pay the balance of his debts ~ a substantial £8,400.

The Hall then was less than thirty years old, a typical Elizabethan manor house set around a quadrangle. Much of its fabric came from the Augustinian priory that had stood here from the days of Henry II until the Dissolution of the Monasteries. The character of that Elizabethan mansion is most apparent today in the Long Gallery with its notable chimneypiece and painted overmantel. Here, along with family portraits, are some curious mementoes like the sturdy gaming-table and chair found in a hollow oak tree at Astley nearby. Tradition says it was used by the Duke of Suffolk, father of Lady Jane Grey, when he was in hiding in 1554.

John Newdegate's move to Arbury failed to solve his financial problems. Nor did his son's marriage to Anne Fitton, daughter of the rich and powerful Sir Edward Fitton, provide the help he needed. John was thrown into a debtor's prison and there he died in 1594.

His son, also named John, was a man of very different mettle. He laboured unceasingly to pay off his father's debts and to make the estate

The Saloon

pay its way. His father-in-law was impressed and bought him one of the knighthoods that James I had put up for sale. The family's fortunes continued to improve when the estate passed to Sir John's second son, Richard Newdigate. (The variations on the spelling of the family name deserve a monograph of their own).

Richard rose to become Chief Justice under Cromwell and was later created a Baronet by Charles II ~ the first man to be so elevated without paying for the honour. It was his son, also Sir Richard, who built the handsome stables at Arbury. The striking central bay with its curved gables was designed by Sir Christopher Wren ~ an account preserved at Arbury records that the celebrated architect received a pair of silver candlesticks, valued at £11, for his work.

Sir Richard also commissioned the eminent plasterer Edward Martin of London 'to seell the chappell at Arbury with ffrettworke seelling', all for £39. Martin spent four years creating this astonishing ceiling, densely decorated with swags of fruit and foliage surmounted by cherubs' heads.

But the man who was to transform Arbury from a traditional Elizabethan mansion to a dazzling Gothick extravaganza was the 5th Baronet, Sir Roger. He succeeded to the title and estate in 1734 when he was only 14 and was to reign at Arbury for 72 years. In 1750 he began to refurbish the interior in the Gothic style, a joyously theatrical display of soaring fan vaults, plunging pendants and the kind of filigree tracery once memorably compared to 'petrified lace'. In the Saloon Sir Roger installed a gloriously decorated bay window and a magnificent ceiling inspired by Henry VII's Chapel in Westminster Abbey; in the Drawing Room, a sumptuous chimney piece based on the canopy of the 13th century tomb of Aymer de Valence, also in Westminster Abbey.

Most dramatic of all is the Dining Room. It was originally the Elizabethan Great Hall and the greater height allows the fan vaulting to appear at its most effective. Around the walls niches, surmounted by elaborate canopies, contain copies of classical statues and between the niches hang some fine Elizabethan and Jacobean portraits, amongst them a particularly striking painting of Queen Elizabeth by John Bettes.

It was of this room that a famous Victorian author was to write: 'It impressed one with its architectural beauty, like a cathedral.... richly carved pendants, all of creamy white relieved here and there by touches of gold'. The author was George Eliot who, as Mary Ann Evans, was born in 1819 at South Farm on the Arbury estate where her father was the steward. Sir Roger had died just over a decade earlier but he and his works would still have been avidly discussed. In *Scenes from Clerical Life*, published in 1857, George Eliot transmutes Arbury into 'Cheverel Manor' and Sir Roger becomes Sir Christopher Cheverel but there is no mistaking their true identities as the author describes how 'Cheverel Manor was growing from ugliness into beauty' under 'Sir Christopher's' direction.

Sir Roger's alterations ended in 1805 and Arbury has scarcely changed since, providing the most breathtaking and complete example of early Gothick Revival architecture in the country. The house's attractions are enhanced by its collections of fine paintings, ~ works by Lely, Lawrence, Reynolds and Romney amongst them ~ , furniture, glass and china accumulated over the centuries by successive generations of the Newdegate family.

Arbury Hall

Broughton Castle

'One of the most fascinating buildings in the county' ~ Arthur Mee

As you cross the ancient bridge over a moat and approach the sturdy 14th century gatehouse, it becomes clear that Broughton Castle is something special. Pass through the gatehouse into the grassed quadrangle and there, rising three storeys high, is the perfect picture of a great Tudor mansion. This north front, with its lofty oriel windows, gabled roofs and tall chimneys, certainly is Tudor but actually a 'modernisation' effected in 1554 on a mansion that was already two and a half centuries old.

The original manor house was built in about 1300 by Sir John de Broughton, who also channelled three streams into the broad moat that covers a full three acres. The greater part of Sir John's house still stands. Its medieval pedigree is evident in the magnificent Great Hall, in the Groined Passage where ribbed vaults stand on strangely-carved corbels, and in the vaulted Dining Room, formerly an undercroft, a dramatically-designed space once used as a store-room.

The Broughton family sold the Castle in 1377 to William of Wykeham, Bishop of Winchester, Chancellor of England, the founder of Winchester School and New College, Oxford. On William's death in 1404, Broughton passed to his great-nephew, Sir Thomas Wykeham, a hero of Agincourt whose sumptuous alabaster effigy lies in the church just beyond the gatehouse. Another warrior who distinguished himself at Agincourt was James Fiennes, later 1st Baron Saye & Sele, and in 1448 the Fiennes (pronounced 'Fines') and the Wykehams were united when James' son married Sir Thomas Wykeham's granddaughter. Their descendants have lived at Broughton ever since. The present owner,

The Great Hall

Nathaniel Fiennes, 21st Lord Saye & Sele, is the latest scion of a family that has been in continuous ownership of the Castle for more than 600 years.

Incredibly, during those six centuries, there has been only one major alteration to the medieval house. That took place in the 1550s when Richard, the 6th Baron, began transforming Broughton into a Tudor mansion. Two storeys were added above the Great Hall, great oriels replaced the narrow Gothic windows and the medieval kitchens were removed to make way for two superb rooms ~ the Oak Room and the Great Parlour.

At the same time, the 6th Baron installed the striking fireplaces: imposing structures in the English style in the Oak Room and Queen Anne's Room, and a very un-English chimneypiece in the King's Chamber. French in inspiration, it has a lovely central panel showing dryads dancing round an oak ~ very similar in style to fireplaces which are known to have been made for Henry VIII's Nonsuch Palace but of which none have survived.

The work of embellishment was continued by the 7th Baron. He added the dazzling plaster ceilings in the main rooms, most notably in the Great Parlour where at one end he records the date, 1599, at the other the initials REF ~ Richard and Elizabeth Fiennes.

Their son, William, an earnest Puritan, was to become one of the leading figures on the Parliamentary side during the Civil War. He had been created a Viscount by James I who stayed at Broughton with his Queen, Anne of Denmark in 1604. (Their rooms are now known as the King's Chamber and Queen Anne's Room, the latter containing a contemporary portrait of the Queen). But soon after the accession of Charles I, William became disenchanted with the new King's despotic ideas. Together with Hampden, Pym and Lord Brooke, he struggled to assert Parliament's supremacy.

The group met frequently at Broughton, ostensibly as the Providence Island Company, an enterprise dedicated to establishing Puritan colonies in America. They did in fact found one settlement at the mouth of the Connecticut river which they named Saybrook after the Lords Saye and Brooke. According to one tradition, William seriously considered emigrating himself until it was pointed out that there was no place for hereditary titles in that brave new world.

The conspirators planned their strategy in a small room at the top of the west stairs. Here can be seen some of the cannonballs recovered from the moat after Broughton was besieged and captured by the Royalists in 1642, while in the Great Hall there's a fine display of Civil War arms and armour. Despite his opposition to the King's policies, William refused to endorse his execution and at the Restoration 'Old Subtlety' as he became known was made a Privy Councillor and pardoned. That pardon can be seen in the Great Parlour along with the original Grant of Barony given in 1447 by Henry VI whose elegant seal is still attached.

Quieter times followed in the 18th century but during Regency times Broughton was imperilled by the wastrel extravagance of William Thomas, son of the 14th Baron and a crony of the Prince Regent. A visitor in 1819 noted that the rooms were 'daily dilapidating from misuse' and in 1837 most of the Castle's contents were disposed of in an eight day sale. Even the swans on the moat were sold.

The family's straitened circumstances during the 19th century had the happy consequence that there were no funds to indulge the Victorian passion for restoring old houses in a mock-medieval style. Broughton Castle has survived as a genuine medieval and Tudor mansion, a dwelling imbued with that indefinable atmosphere unique to houses lived in by generations of the same family.

Coughton Court

'During the six centuries that the Throckmorton family has lived here, Coughton Court has provided a serene backdrop for bloodshed, riot, religious defiance ~ and treason'.

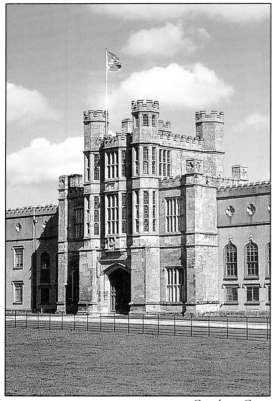

Coughton Court

It seems the perfect expression of harmony and order, this ancient house with its gables, half-timbered walls and dignified gatehouse. But the overwhelming sense of peace is deceptive: during the six centuries that the Throckmorton family has lived here, Coughton Court has provided a serene backdrop for bloodshed, riot, religious defiance ~ and treason.

The family first attained national eminence in the early 1400s when John de Throckmorton rose to become Chamberlain of the Exchequer under Henry VI. Later that century, John's grandson Robert was knighted by Henry VII on the same day in 1494 as the King's son, the future Henry VIII. It seems likely that it was Robert who began building the present Coughton Court, as well as the church nearby in which he placed a splendid tomb for himself. He was never laid to rest in it, dying in Italy during the course of a pilgrimage to the Holy Land.

His son, Sir George, displayed the high principles and refusal to compromise that were to embroil the family in trouble during the succeeding centuries. When Henry VIII was seeking a divorce in order to marry Anne Boleyn, Sir George bluntly accused the King of having 'meddled both with the mother and the sister'. Henry replied mildly, 'Never with the mother'. After Anne Boleyn's Coronation, Sir George deemed it prudent to retire to Coughton and it was probably then that the 'stately castle-like Gate-house of freestone' was built.

After 20 years of opposing the King's Protestant reforms, Sir George died in 1553, ironically the same year in which the Catholic Queen Mary succeeded to the throne. By an even greater irony, his fourth son, Sir Nicholas, was an ardent Protestant and had unwisely made public his objections to the Queen's marriage to King Philip of Spain. He was arrested on a charge of treason but defended himself so eloquently that the jury declared him innocent. Cheated of Sir Nicholas as their victim, the court turned on the members of the jury ~ they were all committed to jail where they languished for several months.

Under Elizabeth, Sir Nicholas returned to royal favour, acting as an emissary to Mary, Queen of Scots, 'by whose beauty he was fascinated'. One of the most poignant of the exhibits at Coughton Court is the white chemise the doomed Queen was wearing at her execution in 1587. Other members of the Throckmorton family remained staunchly loyal to the Old Faith and Coughton Court became a refuge for recusant Catholics. The ingeniously concealed Priest's Room, complete with a palliasse bed, a rope ladder and a folding leather altar was rediscovered during restoration work in 1858.

The Throckmortons Catholic sympathies made them suspect at court and the family's reputation suffered a further reverse when Sir Nicholas' daughter, Bess, a lady-in-waiting to Queen Elizabeth, secretly married Sir Walter Raleigh, a breach of court etiquette for which they were both sent to the Tower.

Still worse was to come in 1605 when Coughton Court became the headquarters of the conspirators in the Gunpowder Plot. Thomas Throckmorton was not living at Coughton that year and was not implicated, but the man to whom he had rented the house, Sir Everard Digby, and the leader of the plot, his nephew Robert Catesby, were both gruesomely executed.

The Civil War brought new tribulations. The Parliamentary forces bombarded the house with cannon and when they were finally driven out, set it on fire. For twenty years Coughton Court stood empty. Then, during the 1660s, the 2nd Baronet, Sir Francis, restored the house, ~ complete with an illegal Catholic chapel, ~ just in time for the anti-Catholic riots of 1688. A mob from Alcester burned down the east wing where the Chapel was situated and ever since then the great quadrangle has remained three-sided.

At this point, happily, the litany of misfortune comes to a close, although the Throckmortons were to endure a further century of persecution for their allegiance to the Roman Catholic faith. Nowadays, Coughton's troubled past is belied by the sense of peace that impresses every visitor to its dignified rooms, to the lovely courtyard with its knot garden layout and to the Walled Garden with its unique rose labyrinth.

The Throckmortons' long and historic tenure of Coughton is mirrored in the outstanding collection of family portraits dating from Tudor times to the present. One of the most dazzling is the portrait of Sir Robert, the 4th Baronet, by Nicolas de Largillière that hangs in the Drawing Room. Sir Robert held the title for 71 years, from 1720 to 1791, outliving his son so that the succession passed to his grandson, Sir John.

A friend of the poet William Cowper, host to the Prince Regent (who came for breakfast one September morning in 1806), and responsible for finalizing building improvements started by the fourth Baronet, Sir John also created one of the family's most popular mementoes. In June, 1811 he wagered a thousand guineas that a team of workers on his Berkshire estate, Buckland, could make 'a coat from the wool which was on the sheep's back at 5.00 a.m. before 9.00 at night'. In fact the coat was ready before half past six that evening and is now on display in the Saloon close to a portrait of Sir John himself that hangs above the fireplace.

The Saloon

Eastnor Castle

'A Castle! Yes! Now that'll stun 'em / No self-respecting Lord's without 'un
It is the perfect acquisition / For someone in my position'
~ Sarah Hervey-Bathurst on Baron Somers, builder of Eastnor Castle

On June 23rd 1812, 'in the presence of many neighbouring gentlemen and their families' John Cocks, 2nd Baron Somers, laid the foundation stone of Eastnor Castle. Beneath it he placed *'a piece of money of Queen Elizabeth (I believe half a crown) my family having settled in Eastnor in that reign; and also a three shilling bank token of the year 1811'*. Beginning with these trifling sums, Lord Somers' Castle was eventually to cost him a total of £83, 923. 13s 11½d ~ about £9 million in today's money.

The expense was worth it. By 1824 Baron Somers (now the 1st Earl Somers) had taken up residence in a memorably romantic Castle, beautifully set overlooking the Malvern Hills, its massive Norman proportions recalling the great fortresses established along these Welsh borders during the reign of Edward I. But even for such a great landowner and successful politician as Lord Somers the enormous expenditure proved crippling, leaving him without the wherewithal to complete his ambitious plans for the interior. The great mock-medieval pile remained genuinely medieval in its Spartan lack of decoration.

Happily, the 2nd Earl rehabilitated the family fortunes by good management, and by good judgement he then called upon the services of A.W.N. Pugin, the young designer whose decoration and sculpture for the new House of Lords had created a sensation. At Eastnor, Pugin created something equally spectacular: a vast Drawing Room that is perhaps the most full-blooded expression of the High Gothic Revival style, and certainly the best surviving example of his domestic work.

In this one gorgeous room, Pugin deployed almost the entire stock of the Gothic Revival

The Long Library

Eastnor Castle

inventory: elaborately-gilded fan tracery, brilliantly-patterned coloured tiles, richly-carved woodwork, an ornate chandelier modelled on a medieval original in Nuremberg Cathedral. Multi-coloured shields and devices celebrate the Earl's family tree in a riot of heraldry that reaches its climax in the dazzling chimneypiece and overmantel where, without a hint of irony, is blazoned the Somers' family motto, *Prodesse quam conspici* ~ Be useful rather than conspicuous. By contrast, Pugin's design fee, a one-off payment of £20, seems decidedly *in*conspicuous.

Shortly after the Drawing Room was completed in 1852, Pugin died, barely 40 years old; three weeks later the 2nd Earl was also dead. His successor, Charles, the 3rd Earl, inherited at a time when the family's prosperity reached its zenith. The Somers' estates sprawled across 13,000 acres of Herefordshire, Worcestershire and Gloucestershire: they also owned the rapidly developing area of Somers Town in Islington, north London. It was time for Charles to embark on a major programme of redecorating the rest of the castle, many of whose rooms were still sparsely furnished.

Afflicted with what he called 'armouritis', Charles was a compulsive buyer of medieval armour and in the 1870s acquired half of the legendary Meyrick Collection. Most of the pieces ~ some of which date back to the early 1500s ~ are now on display in the Red Hall, but originally they were placed in the cavernous Great Hall, 60ft long and 55ft high, appropriate set-dressing for its medieval austerity. Today,

the Hall is furnished as an Edwardian drawing-room, the elephantine ottoman, sofas and armchairs dwarfed by its vast proportions.

A crisp pen-portrait of the 3rd Earl is provided by the wife of Eastnor's present owner, Sarah Hervey-Bathurst, in a verse introduction to the Castle's guide-book: *'He was artistic, sensitive and clever / He loved to paint, but this endeavour / Was forbidden by his mother. / She said to him 'It is not done. / You are a lord, behave like one'*. The Earl's cultural interests however did not go unfulfilled. He married the lovely Virginia Pattle (*'Society said she was not smart / But she was more ~ a work of art'*): Virginia's sister was the pioneering photographer Julia Margaret Cameron, some of whose works are on display at Eastnor.

Their social circle included Tennyson, Browning and Ruskin, Dickens, George Eliot and Thackeray, but the Earl's closest friend was probably the painter G. F. Watts whom he had known since their schooldays together. Charles acquired several of his friend's paintings, including one of the actress Ellen Terry to whom Watts was briefly married, and these now hang in the elegant Octagon Room. The most haunting is a portrait of Charles' wife, Virginia, painted by Watts before the couple met. Charles saw the painting in Watts' studio, fell in love with it and subsequently with the pre-Raphaelite beauty herself.

Charles died in 1883 just as the great agricultural depression heralded the end of the landed aristocracy's Golden Age. Two World Wars, the Wall Street crash of 1929, death duties and the punitive taxation of the mid-1900s all contributed to diminishing the family's wealth and the extent of the estate. When James Hervey-Bathurst, (a descendant of Charles Cocks, the 1st Baron Somers), inherited Eastnor in 1986 the estate had been reduced to 5,000 acres and limited money had been spent on the Castle's decoration for more than fifty years, although great efforts had been made to keep the roof reasonably weatherproof.

Together with his wife Sarah, James Hervey-Bathurst set about an energetic restoration of the Castle. Furniture was retrieved from attics and cellars where it had been stored since the second World War, tapestries and textiles bought and hung, the mid-Victorian splendour triumphantly renewed. As *Country Life* magazine observed in 1993, 'Today Eastnor is in better shape and probably looks more attractive than it ever has before'.

Ragley Hall

'The 3rd Marquess of Hertford was a rich, charming and brilliantly intelligent man, as assiduous and extravagant in his pursuit of pleasure as the Prince Regent himself'

Approaching Ragley Hall through its 400 acres of parkland, the imposing building with its great portico clearly proclaims that here is a Stately Home of consequence. Even so, nothing quite prepares you for the awesome proportions of the first room you enter, ~ the Great Hall, 70ft long, 40ft wide and 40ft high. Its superb baroque decoration was designed by James Gibbs in 1750, the centrepiece a dramatic representation of Minerva riding the clouds in a chariot drawn by two winged lions. Slightly worrying is the fact that the fearsomely long spear she carries is kept in place only by the grip of her plaster hand.

This resplendent Hall stood at the heart of the great house designed by Robert Hooke in the 1670s for the Earl of Conway, Secretary of State to Charles II. Following the fashion of the time, its plan was a model of symmetry with four self-contained apartments, one at each corner, the Hall flanked by a grand Saloon (or Dining Room), Library and Chapel.

The Earl's great-grandfather had bought the Ragley estate some hundred years earlier, and that proved to be the last occasion on which Ragley changed hands by purchase, although the succession has not always been straightforward. When the Earl died soon after Ragley Hall was completed, for example, the estate passed to his only daughter, Laetitia. She was engaged to her cousin, Popham Seymour, but before their wedding day Popham was killed in a duel and Laetitia died shortly afterwards.

Popham's younger brother, Francis Seymour, inherited and the Seymour family have lived at Ragley Hall ever since. Since 1793, they have borne the title of Marquess of Hertford and it was the present 8th Marquess who in 1991 gave the great house and its estate to his son, the Earl of Yarmouth. A farmer by training, the Earl manages the 6000 acres immediately around the house.

Many family photographs and mementoes are scattered around the house, but the most flamboyant celebration of the family is the vast mural that flows around the walls and ceiling of the South Staircase Hall. Designed and painted between 1969 and 1983 by Graham Rust, its subject is the temptation of Christ by the Devil. On the flat ceiling, a dazzling *trompe l'oeil* dome opens to reveal Christ on the mountain while on the painted balconies below family members (and their pets) are gathered to witness the scene. Oddly, some visitors find this luminous panorama out of place in such an historic house: most, however, respond to its sunny *joie de vivre* with enthusiasm.

Opinions also diverge about the huge abstract painting that hangs in the North Staircase Hall, a representation of *The Defeat of the Spanish Armada* painted by Ceri Richards in 1964. Its purchase by the present Marquess of Hertford continued the Seymour family's tradition as patrons of the arts, a tradition which has endowed Ragley with such treasures as Kneller's portrait of Popham Seymour Conway (also in the North Staircase Hall), a superb series of portraits by Sir Joshua Reynolds in the Green Drawing Room, equestrian paintings by John Wootton in the Breakfast Room and John Hoppner's portrait of a sumptuously attired Prince Regent in the Dining Room.

Another portrait of the Prince, painted by Sir Thomas Lawrence, hangs in the Prince Regent's Bedroom, a room dominated by an elegant tester bed specially built for 'Prinnie's' first visit to Ragley in 1796. It is curtained with lovely hand-painted silk made in the 17th century and surmounted by the Prince of Wales' badge of feathers. Here the sleeping Prince was aroused one morning with the tragic news that his only child, Princess Charlotte, had died at the age of 21.

The Prince Regent's host on that occasion was Francis Ingram, 2nd Marquess of Hertford, who a few years earlier had commissioned James Wyatt to build the noble portico and staircase on the East Front, and to create two of the loveliest rooms at Ragley ~ the Mauve Drawing Room and the Red Saloon, triumphs of Georgian elegance which remain exactly as they were designed by Wyatt.

The royal friendship continued into the next generation. Francis Charles, 3rd Marquess of Hertford, was a 'rich, charming and brilliantly intelligent' man, as assiduous and extravagant in his pursuit of pleasure as the Prince Regent himself. 'It would be charitable to assume an element of insanity in Hertford's later excesses' intoned one critic, but this Regency rake was also an art connoisseur whose purchases form the basis of the Wallace Collection in Hertford House, London. He was fortunate too in his marriage to Maria Fagniani, the daughter of an Italian Marchesa. Maria became extremely wealthy when both the Duke of Queensberry and George Selwyn left her their fortunes, 'each believing that she was his daughter'.

During its long history Ragley has suffered periods of neglect ~ the 4th Marquess, for example, preferred to lead a bachelor existence at Bagatelle in Paris and during World War II the 8th Marquess and his mother were confined to the exquisite Library while the rest of the house was commandeered as a hospital. Now fully restored to its former state of grace, the house, together with its spacious grounds, Adventure Wood, Maze, Stables, Carriage Collection and other attractions provides 'something for all of the family, all of the time'.

The East Front

Stanway House

'Only once in almost thirteen centuries has the Manor of Stanway changed hands by purchase'

This enchanting house is surely one of the most perfect of Cotswold mansions. Built using the warm, honey-coloured local stone, surrounded by gardens and landscaped grounds, Stanway House is a dwelling-place at peace with the world and with itself. A towering bay window looks across a scene where for centuries the only changes have been those ordained by the passing of the seasons.

Nearby stands a great Tithe Barn, even older than the house. It was built in 1370 when the Manor of Stanway was a small satellite of Tewkesbury Abbey. Here, four monks absorbed themselves in prayer for the souls of the two Saxon nobles, Odo and Dodo, who had presented the land to the Abbot in 715 AD. Eight centuries later, the then Abbot, anticipating the Dissolution of the Monasteries, leased the manor and so cheated Henry VIII's grasping Commissioners of a valuable property.

The lease of the Manor was bought by Richard Tracy M.P. ~ the only time in nearly 1300 years that the house has changed hands by purchase. The present owners of Stanway, Lord and Lady Neidpath, can trace their descent back to Richard Tracy's father, Sir William Tracy, and beyond.

The Great Hall

The Tracys were a prominent Gloucestershire family who had proved themselves to be persistent thorns in the flesh of a corrupt church. A 12th century ancestor was Sir William de Traci, one of the four knights who murdered Thomas à Becket in Canterbury Cathedral. More recently, Richard's father, Sir William, had declared in his will that he relied on his faith for salvation, not on the prayers of monks. Chancellor Parker of Worcester responded to this slur on the Church by having Sir William's body exhumed and burnt. And Richard himself, charged with dissolving the Abbey of Hailes nearby, outraged the monks by examining the content of their sacred relic, reputedly a phial of the Holy Blood, and declaring that it was duck's blood with a tint of saffron.

It was Richard's son, Sir Paul Tracy who began re-building Stanway around 1580 along the lines of a great Elizabethan manor house. At its heart is the Great Hall whose function changed by the hour ~ from business room to manorial court to dining room. The raised dais on which the Lord of the Manor and his family took their meals is still in place, lit from one side by the floor-to-ceiling bay window, its mullions and transoms channelling the immense intake of light through sixty different segments.

Here, as elsewhere throughout the house, objects both priceless and mundane bear witness to the varied interests of earlier generations. The Hall contains fine paintings in abundance but also a wonderful 23ft long table, shaped from a single piece of oak and designed specifically for that most popular of 17th century parlour games ~ shuffleboard. The game still survives, in a pitifully degraded form, as 'shove ha'penny' but Stanway's shuffleboard is the genuine article, still in full working order and complete with its original brass counters.

One wonders which member of the family thought it advisable to use another of the curiosities in the Hall ~ an Exercising Chair made around 1780 by Thomas Chippendale. It was claimed that half an hour spent bouncing on its leather-covered springs greatly enhanced one's health, if not one's dignity.

These primitive aids to working out were apparently quite common, but two other examples of Chippendale's work, in the Drawing Room next door, are believed to be unique. The two 'Chinese Chippendale' day beds, best described as chaises-longues with four-postered canopies, were presumably created for the 'pale and interesting' valetudinarian ladies who flourished ~ if that's the right word ~ during the heyday of the Romantic Movement.

These unusual pieces were made around 1760 for Arnisfield in East Lothian the seat of the 7th Earl of Wemyss, and the reason why they are now installed at Stanway takes one through some complicated paths of British genealogy. In essence, the male line of the Stanway Tracys died out in 1773 and the estate devolved to the last surviving daughter, Susan. In 1771, Susan married Lord Elcho, son of the 7th Earl of Wemyss, and ever since then Stanway has been lived in by either the Earl of Wemyss or, as at present, by his heir.

One has to be grateful to both families, the Tracys and the Earls of Wemyss, that neither succumbed to the rebuilding fervour of Georgian and Victorian times. The splendid Gatehouse, built around 1630 and 'one of Gloucestershire's architectural gems', still stands unmarred, a building so noble that it was consistently attributed to Inigo Jones. It's now ascribed to a local man, Timothy Strong of Barrington, who went on to become Christopher Wren's favourite mason during the rebuilding of London after the Great Fire.

The Estate Houses have also survived intact and the sense of continuity at Stanway is heightened every Quarter Day when tenants come to the Audit Room to pay their rents. The rent table, made around 1780, has on its square pedestal a revolving top with drawers marked with the letters of the alphabet in which individual rent books were placed and a secret compartment for banknotes. Such visits to the manor house were almost universal before 1914, but Stanway is now one of very few estates still cleaving to this time-honoured tradition.

Stanway

Sudeley Castle and Gardens

'Sir Thomas Seymour was a man of boundless ambition who within hours of Henry VIII's death was proposing marriage to the 15-year-old Princess Elizabeth'

Queen Katherine Parr's Tomb

No fewer than five Queens of England came to know this grand old castle, set in the heart of the Cotswolds. Catherine of Aragon and the ill-fated Anne Boleyn stayed at Sudeley, and the third Queen ~ the 'gracious, learned and pious' Katherine Parr, last wife of Henry VIII, is actually buried here. Witty and eloquent, Katherine had captivated the ageing King and by all accounts their three and a half years of marriage were remarkably happy. But scarcely six weeks after Henry's death Katherine had married again: her new husband was Sir Thomas Seymour, Lord High Admiral of England and Lord of Sudeley Castle.

Uncle of the new King, Edward VI, Sir Thomas was 'aggressively masculine, utterly selfish and, to most women, irresistible'. He was also a man of boundless ambition who within hours of Henry's death was proposing marriage to the 15-year-old Princess Elizabeth. She turned him down. Four days later, Sir Thomas and Katherine became lovers: within a few weeks they were married. Katherine may not have been Sir Thomas' first choice, but the ruthless politician proved to be a kind and considerate husband.

He spent lavishly on preparing Sudeley Castle for his bride and her retinue of some 200 people, building a complete new suite of apartments for her use. When Katherine became pregnant towards the end of 1547, she personally supervised the decoration of the

Nursery. This lovely room contains some exquisite miniatures (including one of Katherine herself) and boasts a superb Tudor stone window looking out over what is now the Queen's Garden, planted with hundreds of varieties of old fashioned roses and aromatic herbs.

Their child, a daughter, was born on August 30th, 1548, but three days after the birth Katherine contracted puerperal fever and died. Henry VIII's dying wish was that she would be interred beside him in the Royal Vault at Windsor but Katherine insisted on burial in the Castle Church at Sudeley where her remains lie beneath a splendid Victorian marble effigy.

Amongst the mourners at Katherine's funeral was a strikingly beautiful girl, then eleven years old. Lady Jane Grey had been a protegée of the Queen and now Sir Thomas schemed to get her married to Edward VI. His plot came to grief when his own brother, the Lord Protector Somerset, indicted him on 33 counts of treason and himself signed the warrant of execution. On a chill February morning five years later, Lady Jane, still only 17, followed him to the executioner's block.

There are happier associations with the last Queen who stayed at Sudeley. Elizabeth I was entertained by the new owner, Giles, Lord Chandos, on three occasions. The most extravagant hospitality was dispensed in 1592 to mark the fourth anniversary of the Spanish Armada's defeat. In commemoration of that visit, the present owner, Lady Ashcombe, has planted that favourite feature of Elizabethan pleasure-grounds, a Knot Garden, its design inspired by the pattern on a dress the Queen is wearing in the portrait that hangs in the Castle.

Half a century after Elizabeth's visit, Sudeley was to suffer drastically during the Civil War. The Chandos family were loyal Royalists and the Castle became the headquarters of the dashing, but militarily inept, Prince Rupert of the Rhine. Three times the Castle was besieged by Cromwell's troops, and three times it was taken. It's still possible to see where one of many cannonballs smashed through the wall of the Octagon Tower.

In 1643, between the second and third of these sieges, the Castle provided a refuge for Charles I himself following his defeat at Gloucester. The spectacular bed in which the King slept is one of Sudeley's greatest treasures, together with the well-known portrait of him by Van Dyck.

Sudeley Castle

In the aftermath of the Civil War, Cromwell ordered that the Castle be 'slighted', or rendered useless for military purposes. His troops were not content with just dismantling Sudeley's defences: the magnificent 15th century Banqueting Hall and the Tithe Barn were also left in ruins. Today, surrounded by gardens, they have a romantic charm but their devastation ~ and the financial penalties imposed on the Chandos' family ~ meant that for the next 180 years Sudeley Castle was to stand empty and abandoned.

For a period in the early 1800s Sudeley was put to use as a livery stables and inn, *The Castle Arms*, and then in 1837 the whole estate was bought by two bachelor brothers, John and William Dent, of the famous Worcestershire glove-making family. Sudeley has remained with their descendants ever since. The brothers used their considerable wealth to restore the Castle, furnishing many of the rooms with pieces bought at the famous Strawberry Hill sale when the contents of Horace Walpole's great Gothic House were auctioned off.

Sudeley was inherited by John and William's nephew, John Coucher Dent, and his energetic wife, Emma. An insatiable collector, Emma filled the Castle with her acquisitions, and also added a North Tower in the 1880s. This contains her bedroom and many of her purchases, their Victorian setting still perfectly preserved. An exhibition at the Castle chronicles the life of this engaging matriarch who was also a diligent diarist and an enthusiastic collector of autographs ~ amongst the many notable figures whose signatures she obtained are Charles Darwin, Florence Nightingale, Sir Walter Scott and Presidents Lincoln and Jackson. Also included in the display is the pedometer Emma strapped to her shoe to record the number of miles she walked each year.

Map B ~ The Costwolds and Oxfordshire

Tewkesbury

M5

B4077

Winchcombe

A417

A38

B4632

Stow-on-the-

Cheltenham

14. Whittington C

A40

Gloucester

A436

A40

A48

A46

A429

M5

A417

A435

A38

COTSWO

Stroud

A419

12. Owlpen Manor

Cirencester

Dursley

B4014

THE

I

Uley

A433

8. Berkeley Castle

10. Chavenage

A419

Tetbury

A46

A433

B4014

A429

M4

M4

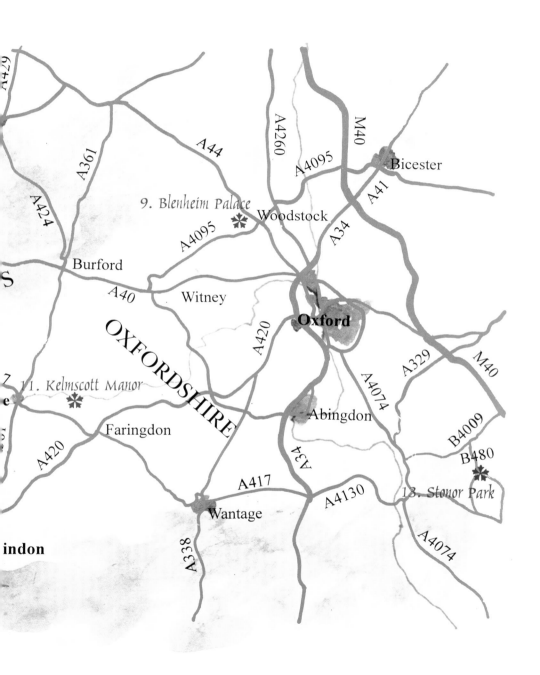

A429

A424

A361

A44

A4260

A4095

M40

Bicester

9. Blenheim Palace

A4095

Woodstock

A41

A34

Burford

A40

Witney

OXFORDSHIRE

A420

Oxford

A329

M40

7 11. Kelmscott Manor

e

A4074

B4009

Faringdon

Abingdon

B480

A420

A34

13. Stonor Park

A417

A4130

indon

A338

Wantage

A4074

Berkeley Castle

Berkeley's towers appear in martial pride,
Menacing all around the champaign wide,
Right famous as the seat of barons bold
And valiant earls whose great exploits are told.
~ Michael Drayton

The murder of King Edward II at Berkeley Castle in 1327 still excites compassion, despite the fact that Edward was certainly one of England's most incompetent monarchs. During his twenty year reign, he managed to lose all the Scottish lands conquered by his father. He incensed the powerful barons by his reliance on favourites such as Piers Gaveston. He earned the contempt of his Queen, Isabella, and it was she, aided by her brother the French King, who toppled Edward from his throne.

The vanquished King was placed in the custody of Thomas, 8th Baron Berkeley and despatched to the Baron's great fortress overlooking the Severn and the Welsh border. Today, as one stands in the room where Edward was imprisoned, it is easy to imagine the horror of his plight. In one corner is the infamous Dungeon, a well 28ft deep into which the rotting carcasses of cattle were thrown. They were followed by the living bodies of prisoners who were left to die by asphyxiation from the fumes. As royalty, Edward was spared this particular atrocity. Instead, he was brutally murdered by his two jailors, Sir John Maltravers and Sir Thomas Gurney.

Lord Berkeley was not involved in this horrible crime, indeed he had earlier been reprimanded for the lenient treatment of his prisoner. Such civility was characteristic of the Berkeleys ~ in an age of robber barons and feudal ferocity Maurice I (who died in 1190) was known as 'Make-peace', Thomas II (1245-1321) as 'The Wise' and Maurice III (1271-

The Morning Room

Berkeley Castle

crashed through the Keep, taking a huge square bite out of the massive wall. Cromwell later returned the Castle to the Berkeleys, but with a legal stipulation that the breach should never be repaired. It never has been.

Following the Restoration, George, the 8th Baron, was created Earl of Berkeley and in the more peaceable decades that followed the Berkeleys generally pursued the life-style of country squires, tending their estates and cherishing their hounds and horses. It's no surprise to find that pride of place in the Picture Gallery at Berkeley is taken by George Stubbs' painting of a *Groom and Horses;* nearby hangs a scene depicting the *Old Berkeley Hounds* attributed to Ben Marshall.

Many more such treasures are scattered through the Castle. In the Tower Room stands an unusual collection of ebony furniture which, according to tradition, was once owned by Sir Francis Drake. The cabin chest in the King's Gallery was definitely Drake's. Portraits by Van Dyck, Reynolds and Kneller hang above the fine 17th century staircase. The Dining Room table is laid with part of the Berkeleys' superb 18th century silver service. Spectacular Brussels tapestries clothe the walls of the timber-roofed Morning Room. And in the Housekeeper's Room, there's a beautifully designed silver cup said to have belonged to Earl Godwin, the father of King Harold and a former owner of Berkeley Manor.

Most breathtaking of all is the magnificent Great Hall, 62ft long and as high as it is wide. It was built on the site of the original hall in about 1340, the saddle-topped roof altered to its present level in 1497. A notable series of Oudenarde tapestries portraying the story of Queen Esther line the walls, along with family portraits ~ one of them by Gainsborough ~ and a 16th century Screen is remarkable for retaining its original painted decoration.

The Great Hall is a memorable sight, as is the view of the Castle from the meadows or from the end of the Bowling Alley. But of course it's not always the most splendid images that stick in the mind. One visitor might be struck by the old sinks of solid lead in the medieval Kitchen, another by the 7ft-long narwhal tusk in the Great Hall, yet another by the fire instructions posted up on the Buttery wall in Edwardian times. In case of fire, a klaxon horn was to be sounded by the Head of Castle Staff *'who will also send up Rockets. The Butler will at once telephone the Thornbury Fire Brigade on Thornbury Tel. No.1.'*

1326) as 'The Magnanimous'. This family trait appears also in the founder of the Berkeley dynasty, Robert FitzHarding, a wealthy Bristol merchant who helped finance Henry II's campaigns against King Stephen and was rewarded with the Manor of Berkeley.

Here, in 1153, Robert began building his formidable castle using a lovely pink-grey stone quarried from the banks of the Severn. The bulk of the Castle dates back to this time, ~ the few additions that *were* made had all been completed by the late 1300s. Robert didn't stay long at his new castle, retiring to St Augustine's Abbey in Bristol (which he had also built) and dying there in 1170.

Throughout the Middle Ages the Berkeleys maintained their position with great style. In 1303, Thomas ('The Wise') 'kept open Christmas for all comers'; Maurice IV (1330-1368) maintained a private army of 156 men in addition to the usual household staff, and his son, Thomas ('The Magnificent'), provided lavish entertainment at the Castle for another doomed King, Richard II.

The Berkeleys were conscientious warriors ~ Thomas II, for example, fought at Bannockburn when he was already seventy ~ and enjoyed the happy knack of nearly always choosing the winning side. The exception was the Civil War when the Castle was captured by Parliamentary forces after a siege of three days. During the hostilities, a cannon ball

Blenheim Palace

'...one of the most astonishing feats of architecture' ~ Sacheverell Sitwell

Detail from 'Battle of Blenheim' tapestry by de Vos after de Hondt

The Battle of Blenheim on August 13th 1704 was all over in a matter of hours: the battle of Blenheim Palace dragged on for almost twenty years. The first was a glorious victory for the English commander, John Churchill, 1st Duke of Marlborough: the second a series of skirmishes conducted by the Duke's wife, Sarah, against craftsmen, suppliers, decorators, the Duke himself and, most virulently, against the architect Sir John Vanbrugh.

The story started happily enough. After his rout of the French army near the village of Blindheim on the river Danube, Churchill was the darling of the nation. Queen Anne, a close friend of the Churchills, proposed that the English people should show their appreciation by building the Duke a great 'house, castle or palace'. She even provided a site by presenting the Royal Manor of Woodstock at a quit-rent of a copy of the French royal flag in the form of a banner to be presented to the Sovereign each year on the anniversary of the battle. Parliament dutifully followed the Queen's example by voting a huge grant which eventually totalled £240,000.

The Duke was invited to choose his own architect and that was when the troubles started. Sarah wanted to appoint the most revered architect of the age, Sir Christopher Wren. Instead the Duke selected Sir John Vanbrugh, a popular man-about-town and successful playwright, whose first foray into architecture had been to design the monumental Castle Howard in Yorkshire. The Duchess was incensed: the Duke, fortunately, remained adamant. Work began in 1705.

Sarah had wanted a large, but comfortable country house: Vanbrugh envisaged a building on an heroic scale, one that would challenge the grandeur of Louis XIV's palace at Versailles. The sharp-tongued Duchess constantly harassed Vanbrugh with insults and complaints. She was shocked by the 'extravagance' of providing 'Cover'd Ways for Servants' in the Kitchen Court and insisted that less costly stone should be used. When the Plymouth Moor stone that Vanbrugh had prescribed for the entrance stairs took months to arrive, Sarah attributed the delay to malice ~ her architect was deliberately depriving her of a seemly means of entry.

Then, in 1712, the Churchills were suddenly out of favour. The Queen had wearied of Sarah's 'teasing and tormenting' and dismissed her; a new Tory government nullified the Duke's great victories by negotiating the Treaty of Utrecht. Building funds from the Treasury dried up so that all work stopped and craftsmen such as Grinling Gibbons ended up receiving only a third of what was due to them. To add insult to injury, the Duke was then accused of embezzling public monies.

From 1712 to 1714, the Duke and Duchess travelled abroad in what Sarah called 'a sort of exile' but returned to England the day after Queen Anne died. In 1716, work at Blenheim resumed. Surprisingly, Vanbrugh also returned but within a few months there was a final breach with the Duchess and he left in fury. Nine years later, close to death, he and Lady Vanbrugh, together with the Earl of Carlisle and party, presented themselves at the great entrance arch to Blenheim. All were refused admittance, even to the Park. The Duke, (now incapacitated by a stroke), and Sarah had finally taken up residence in 1719 and Sarah was soon complaining that all the cold stone was exacerbating her gout.

In a way, one can understand Sarah's objections. Vanbrugh's Blenheim was never intended to be a family home but an overwhelming statement of national glory, its colossal proportions massed like battle lines. The Great Hall, for example, soars 67ft to a superb painted ceiling by Sir James Thornhill showing the Duke, on bended knee, offering his victory to Britannia, the Spirit of the Nation. (Sir James was also to have painted the ceiling in the Long Library but Sarah believed he had overcharged her and cancelled the commission).

But during her long widowhood of twenty-two years Sarah continued to work on completing the sumptuous decoration of the Palace and revealed a more engaging side of her nature in the huge but touching memorial she erected in the Chapel to her beloved husband. Towards the end of her life the Duke of Somerset proposed marriage to her. She wrote to him: 'If I were young and handsome as I was, instead of old and faded as I am, and you could lay the empire of the world at my feet, you should never share the heart and hand that once belonged to John, Duke of Marlborough'.

A century and a half after the Duke's death, on November 30th, 1874, another of the Titans of British history was born here. 'At Blenheim' declared Sir Winston Churchill in later years, 'I took two very important decisions: to be born and to marry. I am happily content with the decisions I took on both occasions'. For the first few years of his life Churchill was actually heir to the dukedom of Marlborough, a destiny one imagines he would not have welcomed.

Sir Winston was a frequent visitor to Blenheim and the room where he was born contains some fascinating mementoes ~ curls 'cut from his head when he was five', his painting of the Great Hall, a piece of shrapnel that fell between him and his cousin, the 9th Duke, during the First World War, and the famous siren suit he wore in the Whitehall bunker during the Second.

Churchill asked to be buried in the graveyard of Bladon church about a mile away. Appropriately, Vanbrugh's north-south axis for Blenheim runs from Bladon tower, passing through the Great Hall and the Saloon, and on to the Column of Victory on the hilltop. Here Sir Winston's illustrious ancestor, the 1st Duke, stands 134ft above the ground holding aloft a winged Victory 'as an ordinary man might hold a bird'.

Aerial view of Blenheim Palace

Chavenage

'A hearse drew up at the manor house driven by a headless man, and the Colonel was seen to rise from his coffin and enter the carriage after a profound reverence to the headless personage, who as he drove away assumed the shape of the martyr King Charles I' ~ The Legend of Chavenage

There is surely no better introduction to an historic house than to have its owner as your guide. At Chavenage visitors are conducted around the lovely Elizabethan mansion by either David Lowsley-Williams or one of his family, each of them providing a commentary rich in history, anecdote, legend and humour.

The narrative begins with the outside, its appearance virtually unchanged since 1576 when Edward Stephens completed his E-shaped building with its traditional Cotswold gables. Those oddly-assorted stones around the smaller windows ~ 'almost certainly cannibalised from the priory at Horsley, abandoned since the Dissolution of the Monasteries'. And notice the large stone just in front of the doors ~ that was probably from an altar in the priory. It was

Chavenage

common practice to put these stones in front of entrances, thus 'encouraging the populace to tread on Roman superstition'. In the fine old door, note the spy-hole for scrutinising dubious visitors and the many bolts and rings, one of which is a sanctuary ring, again probably from Horsley priory.

Then into the lofty Main Hall with its great windows whose glass was garnered from a variety of sources. A striking roundel showing St John the Baptist's head being presented to Salome is pointed out; over there, to the right, 'an amusing little naked lady' and, near the top, a square sundial . Note also the Minstrel's Gallery, housing an 18th century organ, the early 17th century refectory table, the noble fireplace, and those pillars each side of the double doors. They are actually the posts from a Jacobean bed, the remainder of which is still upstairs.

So, upstairs now to the two tapestry rooms to hear 'The Legend of Chavenage', a macabre story from the days of the Civil War. It was Christmas 1648, the King had been defeated and was in prison, but Cromwell was determined that Charles should be executed. Seeking support for his plans, Cromwell sent Gen. Ireton to persuade the owner of Chavenage, Col. Nathaniel Stephens M.P., to join the regicides. Although Nathaniel had raised a regiment of horse to fight for the Parliamentary side, he was a moderate, mild-mannered man who recoiled from the idea of killing the king. He and Ireton argued through the night until Nathaniel was finally won over.

Nathaniel's daughter, Abigail, was horrified when she learnt of his decision. She laid a curse upon her father and shortly afterwards, so the story goes, the Colonel was taken terminally ill. When all were assembled at the side of his death-bed, 'a hearse drew up at the door of the manor house driven by a headless man, and the Colonel was seen to rise from his coffin and

Cromwell's room

enter the carriage after a profound reverence to the headless personage, who as he drove away assumed the shape of the martyr King Charles I'.

The rooms where General Ireton and Cromwell stayed are both hung with splendid 17th century tapestries and in Ireton's room there's an unusual bed which is thought to be a 'sick-bed' ~ 'note the heavy holes by which it could be hung and swung like a cot'.

Next, the room called Queen Anne's Room in which Princess Marie-Louise, grand-daughter of Queen Victoria, wrote her book *My Memories of Six Reigns.* Across the passage, Cholmondley's Room, used by General Horrocks in 1940 and by the Americans planning the assault on Normandy's Omaha Beach in 1944. Then down the stairs, to pause by a small window in the porch for another romantic tale from Civil War times.

In 1644, when the Roundheads were besieging the Royalist stronghold of Beverstone Castle nearby, it was discovered that a young girl at Chavenage was conducting a secret courtship with the son of the Castle's commander. To let him know that no attack was planned that night, she would place a candle in this window as a signal that they could safely meet. 'On the detection of this subterfuge, a candle was placed in the window and the order given to attack in the knowledge that the commander was away for the night!'

And so the tour continues, each room yielding new anecdotes and information. The beautifully constructed model of a sailing boat was made in 1943 by Italian prisoners-of-war working at Chavenage and given to Mrs George Lowsley-Williams. A photograph of David Lowsley-William's grandfather prompts the observation that he was only the third person in Gloucestershire to own a motor-car. And the bundle of very early aerial photographs of the area? They were taken by pilots of the Australian Flying Corps who were based nearby during World War I and for whom Chavenage became 'open house'.

It's not surprising to find that such a graceful house has been popular with television producers from as far back as 1976. Agatha Christie's *The Mysterious Affair at Styles* was filmed here in 1990 and Chavenage was then chosen as the location for the return of the *Are You Being Served?* cast in a new series called *Grace and Favour.* The house and grounds also featured in *The House of Elliott* and, something of a first for an historic house, has even provided the setting for one of Noël Edmonds' 'Gotchas' in *Noël's House Party.*

Kelmscott Manor

The 'loveliest haunt of ancient peace' that can well be imagined ~ William Morris

The bed in William Morris's Room

'Midsummer in the country: here you may walk between the fields and hedges that are as it were one huge nosegay for you, redolent of bean-flowers and clover and sweet hay and elder-blossom'. William Morris wrote that description of the countryside around Kelmscott in 1889. He was then 55 years old, his reputation assured as a master craftsman who had revolutionised the art of house decoration in England.

The firm that he had founded in 1861 with his Pre-Raphaelite friends, 'Morris, Marshall, Faulkner & Company', produced fabrics and furniture inspired by a renewed respect for the simple materials and craftsmen's skills that had been supplanted by Victorian techniques of mass-production.

The firm was based in London but it was to Kelmscott that Morris came for inspiration.

He had grown to love these somnolent villages while an undergraduate at Oxford, exploring them on walking tours with his fellow-student and lifelong friend, Edward Burne-Jones. In 1871, when he was looking for a retreat from the soot and grime of central London, he settled on this sequestered village beside the river Thames, 'a village not so very far from London yet in a country out of the tracks of the busiest people ... with a remote and unchanging air about it that put it beyond dullness'. He and the poet-painter Dante Gabriel Rossetti took out a joint lease on Kelmscott Manor, a charming Elizabethan manor house flanked by a twin-gabled block added a hundred years later.

In his Utopian novel *News from Nowhere* Morris describes arriving at Kelmscott during haymaking time: 'We crossed the road and again almost without my will my hand raised the latch of a door in the wall, and we stood presently on a stone path which led up to the old house ... My companion gave a sign of pleased surprise and enjoyment; nor did I wonder, for the garden between the wall and the house was redolent of the June flowers, and the roses were rolling over one another with that delicious superabundance which at first sight takes away all thought from the beholder save that of beauty. The blackbirds were singing their loudest, the doves were cooing on the roof-ridge, the rooks in the high elm trees beyond were garrulous among the young leaves, and the swifts wheeled whining about the gables. And the house itself was a fit guardian for all the beauty of this heart of summer'. The 'high elm trees' have succumbed to Dutch elm disease, but otherwise the gardens and the lovely Elizabethan manor house, remain virtually unaltered ~ 'the loveliest haunt of ancient peace'.

But the sunny rural idyll was not without its shadows. When William, his wife Jane, and their two daughters came to stay for the first time in June 1871, Rossetti was already in residence. Jane had already modelled several times for him ~ his outstanding portrait of her, *The Blue Silk Dress,* hangs in the Panelled Room at Kelmscott. Rossetti's painterly fascination with Jane's ethereal but sensual beauty seems to have burgeoned into an *amitié amoureuse.* Shortly after delivering his family to Kelmscott, Morris departed for Iceland, writing to his wife, *'Please, dear Janey, be happy'.*

If there was an affair between Rossetti and Jane Morris, it was conducted with the utmost discretion. But the following summer when they gathered again at Kelmscott, Rossetti, grieving for his wife who had died from an overdose of laudanum, suffered a major mental breakdown. Throughout 1873 he lived at Kelmscott as a virtual recluse, suffering delusions, hearing voices, subject to irrational suspicions. Morris, remarking cryptically that Rossetti had 'all sort of ways so unsympathetic to the sweet simple old place', was about to relinquish the lease when Rossetti decided to return to London.

He left behind the enchanting coloured chalk drawings of Morris' two daughters, Jenny, aged 10, and May, aged 9, that now hang in the Panelled Room. They're just two of the many reminders of the family's years at Kelmscott,

Kelmscott Manor

The Panelled Room

a tenure which lasted from 1871 until May's death in 1938. The Green Room, for example, is hung with *Kennet* chintz, designed by Morris in 1883, while the fireplace tiles are patterned with his *Acanthus* design of 1870. In Mrs Morris' Room stands the four-poster bed in which he was born at Walthamstow in 1834, the son of a prosperous City bill-broker.

But perhaps the most striking object in the house is the early 17th century oak four-poster in Morris' own bedroom. It is hung with beautifully-designed hangings and the brilliantly-coloured vallance was expertly embroidered by his younger daughter, May, with his poem *For the bed at Kelmscott.* On the walls hang Dürer's *Melancholia,* Robetta's *Allegory of the power of love* and Mantegna's *Bacchanal, with a wine press,* the vines in which may well have inspired Morris' famous *Vine* design.

Following the death of May Morris in 1938, Kelmscott went through an unhappy period ~ rented out on short-term leases or standing empty for months at a time. (Astonishingly, the 17th century tapestries that William Morris found in place here in 1871 survived this period of neglect and are still in remarkably good condition). Then in 1962 the house passed into the care of the Society of Antiquaries who have restored Kelmscott so sympathetically that one could imagine May Morris once again content with this 'old house which my sister and I consider the only house in England worth inhabiting!'

Owlpen Manor

'Owlpen in Gloucestershire ~ ah, what a dream is there!' ~ Vita Sackville-West

Even in this part of the Cotswolds, where almost every prospect pleases, Owlpen is uniquely lovely, ~ 'a breathtaking ensemble of truly English beauty'. Manor house, church, mill and cottages of pearl-grey stone are framed by a natural amphitheatre of steep, wooded hills, a timeless setting for what the Prince of Wales hailed as 'the epitome of the English village'.

Owlpen's recorded history stretches back for almost a thousand years, but the site was almost certainly inhabited long before that, a settlement attracted here by the springs that rise beneath the house. From about 1100 the estate was owned by the de Olepenne family, local landowners of some consequence. At least ten generations of the de Olepennes succeeded to the manor until, in 1462, Margery, last of the line, married a wealthy merchant, John Daunt. By this time, the Great Barn (now the Cyder Press Restaurant) had been built and part of the east wing of the present house also dates back to this period.

Those were the dislocated days of the Wars of the Roses and the Daunts were closely involved in the Lancastrian interest. A family tradition maintains that Margaret of Anjou, Henry VI's Queen, stayed at Owlpen in May 1471 on her way to the disastrous Battle of Tewkesbury. Margaret only stayed one night, but has since returned many times as a quiet and benevolent ghost. One of the most persuasive sightings occurred during World War II when some children, evacuated from London's East End, were billeted at Owlpen. One night, the then-owner, Barbara Bray, found four of the children awake and excited. They had seen 'a lovely lady with long sleeves and dress all trimmed with fur, and with a funny peaked hat that had a long veil hanging down behind' ~ a convincing description of the Queen's probable costume by children who knew nothing of the legend.

The Queen's real, and spectral, connection with Owlpen is commemorated in Queen Margaret's Room, remarkable for its vivid

Owlpen Manor

The Cyder House

Painted Cloths covering the walls. From around 1350 to the late 1600s these cloths, less expensive than tapestries, were a popular form of decoration. Apart from fragments in provincial museums, few have survived and none of the quality and scale of those at Owlpen.

The actual room that Queen Margaret stayed in was probably demolished during the rebuilding undertaken by Thomas Daunt I. He owned Owlpen between 1542-1574 and built ~ or rebuilt ~ the centre block comprising the present Hall and Great Chamber. These atmospheric, low-ceilinged rooms now contain mostly 17th and early-18th century oak furniture together with an interesting sequence of portraits of the Mander family whose descendants, Nicholas and Karin Mander, have lived at Owlpen since 1974.

The last major changes to the fabric of the manor took place in 1616 when Thomas Daunt II rebuilt the solar wing to the west, made some internal re-arrangements and built the little Court House nearby. Despite this new building, throughout most of the 17th century Owlpen became secondary to the Daunts' estates in Ireland. The last phase of works was an internal remodelling of the east wing by Thomas Daunt V, adding an elegant dovecote, sash windows and a panelled parlour in 1723.

The manor was to slide into neglect when Mary Daunt inherited the estate and married a wealthy industrialist Thomas Stoughton in 1815. They considered the manor too small, old fashioned and uncomfortable and built themselves a grand Italianate mansion at the other end of the estate. For more than a century, Owlpen was demoted to the status of a 'garden house', a place for picnics and excursions. But its shuttered rooms were kept in basic repair and its terraced gardens maintained in good order.

The manor was awakened from its Sleeping Beauty slumbers by a Prince Charming in the form of the architect Norman Jewson. He had discovered this 'beautiful and romantically situated old house' while cycling through the Cotswolds before the First World War and in 1925 purchased it for £3,200. Inspired by the ideals of William Morris, Jewson was a dedicated member of the Society for the Protection of Ancient Buildings and, heeding its principles, displayed exemplary sensitivity in *repairing*, not *restoring*, the venerable building using only traditional skills and methods. Every nail, clout and spike was hand-made; every decorative feature meticulously hand-crafted.

Jewson himself regarded his work at Owlpen as the most satisfying achievement of his career but not long after his repairs were complete he was forced to sell. The new owner was the redoubtable Barbara Bray, 'an unforgettable entertainer, a voluble monologuist, active and jolly'. The old house was once again a family home and busy with guests such as Evelyn Waugh, Peter Scott, her cousin Clive Bell and other members of the 'Bloomsbury group'.

A new chapter in Owlpen's long history opened in 1974 when Nicholas and Karin Mander acquired the manor. They managed to reassemble much of the old estate, buying back farmland, woodland, cottages and outbuildings, many of which have been repaired and restored as holiday cottages. It's pleasing to know that the Manders were befriended by Norman Jewson in his last years ~ the collection at Owlpen of pieces made by members of the Cotswold Arts and Crafts movement seems a fitting tribute to the man who did so much to save what Francis Comstock has called 'By far the most perfect small Manor House in all of England'.

Stonor

*'No house can vie with Stonor for sheer romance, its historic past
and unrivalled position as a stronghold of Catholicism ~ June Ducas*

Stonor Park

For more than 800 years the Stonor family have lived in this secluded valley tucked away in the Chiltern Hills. The first of whom there is any record is Robert de Stanora who died in 1185. From him the succession has passed from father to son with only three exceptions ~ twice when the estate passed to a younger brother, and once to a grandson. The present incumbent, Thomas Stonor, 7th Lord Camoys, represents the 28th generation of the family.

During the first four centuries of their long tenure, the Stonors flourished. They augmented their estates by marrying well ~ at the end of the 14th century Thomas Stonor owned thirty-one manors scattered across the country from East Anglia to Cornwall. The sheep on those estates provided the wool that increased the family's wealth still more. They were also great warriors ~ Stonors fought with honour alongside Edward III at Crecy, with Richard II in Ireland, Henry V in France and for Henry VII at Bosworth and Flodden. At court too they found favour, and not just for the fragrant, thyme-flavoured venison they took there from Stonor park: the family served the Crown variously as Privy Councillors, High Sheriffs of the County, Chief Justices and as Knights of the Body ~ prominent members of the Court who escorted the monarch's body at his funeral.

For much of that time, the house at Stonor was comparatively modest but around 1350 Sir John de Stonore greatly extended it by adding a new Hall, Solar (withdrawing room), Buttery and Kitchen, rooms which, together with the earlier Hall, still form the core of the present building. The Chapel, built of stone and flint, is even older. Services were being held there in 1331 and, without a break, Mass has been celebrated at its altar for more than 650 years.

Another flurry of building activity took place in the 1530s when Sir Walter Stonor linked the rambling medieval buildings together to form the familiar E-shaped Tudor mansion and covered the timber and stone walls with a façade of rose-red brick. The timing was fortuitous for the Stonors had reached the turning-point in their fortunes ~ during the course of the next 300 years these steadfast adherents to the Old Religion would be swept to the margins of English public life, their estates confiscated or sold to pay swingeing fines, their kin persecuted, tortured and even executed.

Dame Cecily Stonor was one of many who displayed an heroic devotion to their faith. In 1577 her annual fine for recusancy was set at the equivalent of £50,000, a staggering penalty which did not deter her from giving sanctuary at Stonor to the Jesuit priest and martyr Edmund Campion. In a secret room in the roof he supervised the printing of his book *Decem Rationes*, 'Ten Reasons for Being a Catholic'.

Dame Cecily's son, John, guided Campion around the Catholic houses of the country but when the clandestine printing press was seized at Stonor both he and his mother were imprisoned for several months. Campion himself was captured at Wantage in July 1581, three times put to the rack, convicted on a bogus charge of conspiracy and executed.

A notable legacy of those troublous times is the collection of recusant books and pamphlets, printed illegally or smuggled in from abroad, housed in Stonor's lovely library with its barrel-vaulted ceiling. There are also many anti-Catholic pamphlets designed to discredit the Papist cause with scurrilous verses such as this: *Friars have power silly nuns to charme / So on a bed they wanton, clip, and kisse / There's nothing in a Nunnery amisse'.*

With greater or less severity the persecution of Catholics continued throughout the 17th and well into the 18th centuries. But by the early 1700s, the Stonors were able to begin replacing the old mullions with the present sash windows, to lay out the formal gardens and, around 1760, to redecorate the medieval Hall and the Chapel in the newly-fashionable Gothic Revival style.

With the Catholic Emancipation Act of 1829, the Stonors immediately bounced back into public life. Thomas Stonor, 3rd Lord Camoys, became Member of Parliament for Oxford, High Sheriff of the County and a Lord in Waiting to Queen Victoria for a record 32 years. It's a tradition of public service that has been continued by the present Lord Camoys who is also a Lord in Waiting to the Queen, a

The Hall

Deputy Lieutenant of Oxfordshire and a Consultor to the Holy See on financial matters.

Despite the long years of oppression, Stonor today presents a serene face to the world. Inside, it numbers amongst its treasures family portraits by Kneller, Hoppner and Gainsborough, some striking works by Ludovico Carracci and two delightful portraits of the children Anne and Elizabeth Hoby by an unknown artist. In Francis Stonor's Bedroom stands a remarkable mahogany bed from around 1830 carved in the shape of a shell floating on the backs of mermaids and dolphins, together with an eye-dazzling set of Venetian grotto chairs made from *limewood.*

The Dining Room is dominated by its exotic wallpaper ~ an early 19th century design showing the great buildings of Paris imaginatively lined up along the bank of the river Seine. Elsewhere you'll discover one of the largest collections of English silhouette portraits, an imposing William and Mary four-poster bed, two very rare Venetian globes dated 1699 and, on a more mundane level, a Victorian rocking-stool specifically designed to provide comfort to sufferers from gout.

Shell-shaped mahogany bed

Whittington Court

On September 9th, 1592, Queen Elizabeth 'dyned at Mr Cotons at Whytington'

The cluster of buildings at Whittington seems to encapsulate the very essence of the Cotswolds. A tiny church, more than seven hundred years old, almost butts on to the house and may well have originally been its chapel. Inside is a fine brass to the memory of Richard Cotton who died in 1556 and whose son, John, is believed to have built the present house.

Whittington's history however stretches much farther back than that. In 'Cow Pasture' just across from the church, the remains of a 2nd-4th century Roman villa were uncovered in 1948 (and subsequently filled in). Nearby were found vestiges of the Anglo-Saxon settlement, recorded as Witetune in the Domesday Book. A little to the north of that can be discerned the outline of medieval Whittington with the existing village of largely 16th to 18th century houses just beyond.

For much of the Middle Ages, the manor of Whittington belonged to the de Crupes family. Three members of that family, two of them attired in chain-mail, are commemorated in the church by recumbent effigies dating from the late 13th and early 14th centuries. At some time in the early 1400s, Whittington became part of the vast estates of the Earl of Gloucester, passing by marriage to, successively, the Earl of Worcester, the Earl of Warwick, and then to the great Richard Neville, 'Warwick the Kingmaker'. His widow was prevailed on by Henry VII to transfer the manor to him and Whittington remained a royal manor until 1545.

Whittington Court and St. Bartholomew's Church

The Library

In that year Henry VIII sold the estate to the Cotton family who were to hold it for more than a hundred years.

It is not known exactly when John Cotton built his new manor house but it was certainly complete by 1592 for on the 9th of September Elizabeth I 'dyned at Mr Cotons at Whytington'. The Queen was making a progress through Gloucestershire, and after her meal at Whittington travelled on to Sudeley Castle for three days of celebrations marking the anniversary of the Spanish Armada's defeat.

Possibly John Cotton's house was designed to be built in the shape of an E, a pattern that satisfied the Elizabethan love of symmetry and was also an ostentatious means of flattering the Queen. But the land around the Court is liable to flooding and it seems possible that the western end of the house was undermined and collapsed. Certainly, later building was concentrated on the eastern side, the additions giving the house its charmingly irregular appearance. These extensions were probably carried out by John's son, Ralph, who in 1614 also built the great barn that does much to enhance Whittington's manorial character.

The most complete part of the early house, its Tudor fireplace still intact, is the former hall, now the Dining Room. An even more impressive fireplace is in the Library, a grand Renaissance chimneypiece that reaches from floor to ceiling. Originally, the carved armorial above the mantel would have been painted, creating a colourful contrast to the stonework. This lovely room with its deep bayed windows forms part of the wing added by Ralph Cotton between 1620 and 1640. The noble three-storey staircase of dark oak that links the new wing with the older part of the house is of this period and has on its first half-landing a carved dog-gate, a very rare survival.

The direct line of the Cottons died out in 1660 and through marriage to one of the Cotton daughters, Whittington was owned for some years by Sir John Denham, a minor poet and major gambler, amateur architect and professional courtier, and Royalist secret agent. After Sir John's death in 1669, Whittington passed through the hands of a bewildering succession of owners and tenants and for most of the 18th century was used as a farmhouse. During this period the pointed finials on the grand staircase were sawn off to avoid snagging the sacks of grain hoisted to the upper floors. But in 1823 the manor was acquired by Walter Lawrence Lawrence, the owner of extensive estates in the area, and the house remained with his family until the last surviving member died in 1985.

Most of the portraits at Whittington are of the Lawrences and include a particularly fine 17th century one of Anthony Lawrence that hangs in the Library. Some of the most important furnishings were brought here from other houses owned by the Lawrences: the panelling in the hallway came from Sevenhampton Manor (a few hundred yards away, just across the A40), the superb Regency bookcase in the Library from Sandywell Park (on the other side of the hill).

In 1985, when Whittington was bequeathed to Mrs Joan Charleston, the house was in a dilapidated condition. Mrs Charleston, together with her husband Robert, daughter and son-in-law undertook an extensive programme of restoration and now the house is once again full of light and interest.

The Dining Hall

ARBURY HALL, NUNEATON, WARWICKSHIRE, CV10 7PT.
(01203) - 382804. Viscount Daventry

Map A: #1. Arbury Hall is on the B4112, about 3m W of Nuneaton, and 4m from Exit 3 of the M6 via the A444. Signposted from the A444. Elizabethan mansion, interior in Gothick Revival style of latter 18th C; Extensive landscaped gardens; Gift Shop; Stables Tea Rooms. DISABLED: *Hall*: Ground Floor only, ramp access to main hall; *Gardens*: Gravel paths difficult for wheelchairs. Disabled visitors may alight at the Hall main entrance before parking in allocated areas.

OPENING TIMES: HALL: 16TH APRIL - 24TH SEPTEMBER: 2.00 p.m. - 5.30 p.m. (Sundays & Bank Holiday Mondays); GARDENS: 2.00 p.m. - 6.00 p.m. (Sundays & Wednesdays). Last admissions to Hall and Gardens: 5.00 p.m. Open for pre-booked parties on most dates, minimum 25 persons.

BERKELEY CASTLE, BERKELEY, GLOUCESTERSHIRE, GL13 9BQ.
(01453) - 810332. Mr & Mrs R.J.G. Berkeley

Map B: #8. Berkeley Castle is in the town of Berkeley, just west of the A38 midway between Bristol & Gloucester. From the M5 use either Exit 14 (5m) or Exit 13 (9m). 12th C Castle, home of the Berkeley family for almost 850 years; Terraced Elizabethan Gardens with lily-pond; Butterfly Farm; Gift Shop; Tea Rooms. DISABLED: In exceptional circumstances, disabled/elderly visitors may alight in the Outer Bailey. No toilet facilities for disabled.

OPENING TIMES: APRIL & MAY: 2.00 p.m. - 5.00 p.m. (Tuesday-Sunday); JUNE & SEPTEMBER: 11.00 a.m. - 5.00 p.m. (Tuesday-Saturday); 2.00 p.m. - 5.00 p.m. (Sunday); JULY & AUGUST: 11.00 A.M. - 5.00 P.M. (Monday-Saturday); 2.00 p.m. - 5.00 p.m. (Sunday); OCTOBER: 2.00 p.m. - 4.30 p.m. (Sundays only). BANK HOLIDAY MONDAYS: 11.00 a.m. - 5.00 p.m. Groups must book in advance.

BLENHEIM PALACE, WOODSTOCK, OXON. OX20 1PX.
(01993) - 811091. The Duke of Marlborough

Map B: #9. The entry to Blenheim Palace is off the A44, 8m N of Oxford. 18th C Palace, home of the 11th Duke of Marlborough and birthplace of Sir Winston Churchill; 2,400-acre Park landscaped by 'Capability' Brown; Italian Garden; Water Terraces. A range of other facilities includes: Motor Launch; Rowing Boats; Marlborough Maze (with Giant Chess & Draughts, and Putting); Lavender & Herb Garden; Butterfly House; Adventure Play Area; Shops; Restaurants; Cafeterias; Extensive Picnicking & Parking areas. DISABLED: Disabled visitors may alight at the Palace entrance. Toilet facilities in both the Palace and the Park.

OPENING TIMES: MID-MARCH - 31ST OCTOBER: 10.30 a.m. - 5.30 p.m. (daily) Last admission: 4.45 p.m. PARK ONLY: 1ST NOVEMBER-MID-MARCH.

BROUGHTON CASTLE, BANBURY, OXFORDSHIRE, OX15 5EB.
(01295) - 262624. Lord Saye and Sele

Map A: #2. Broughton Castle is 5m from Junction 11 of the M40, on the B4035 Banbury - Shipston-on-Stour road, about 2m W of Banbury Cross. Medieval & Tudor mansion (1300-1550); 3-acre Moat; Arms & Armour Collection; Gardens; Park; Gift Shop; Tea Room. DISABLED: Disabled visitors allowed vehicle access to main entrance.

OPENING TIMES: MAY 18TH - 14TH SEPTEMBER: 2.00 p.m. - 5.00 p.m. (Wednesday & Sunday); ALSO: Thursdays in JULY & AUGUST: 2.00 p.m. - 5.00 p.m. BANK HOLIDAY SUNDAYS & MONDAYS, INCLUDING EASTER: 2.00 p.m. - 5.00 p.m. Groups welcome on any day and at any time throughout the year by appointment.

CHAVENAGE, near TETBURY, GLOUCESTERSHIRE, GL8 8XP.
(01666) - 502329.   Fax: (01453) - 836778.   Col. D. Lowsley-Williams

Map B: #10. Chavenage is located 2m NW of Tetbury, signposted from the A4135, B4014, and A46. Elizabethan mansion. Catering by arrangement.

OPENING TIMES: MAY - SEPTEMBER: 2.00 p.m. - 5.00 p.m. (Thursday & Sunday). Also open on Easter Sunday & Monday. Sufficient notice of large groups is essential. Groups of twenty or more are welcomed at any time on any day by prior arrangement.

COUGHTON COURT, ALCESTER, WARWICKSHIRE, B49 5JA.
(01789) - 400777.   Mrs. Clare Throckmorton

Map A: #3. Coughton Court is on the A435, 2m N of Alcester, 15m S of Birmingham. Tudor Mansion set in 25 acres of gardens and grounds; Walled Garden; Gunpowder Plot Exhibition; Children's Clothes Exhibition; Riverside Walk; Gift Shop & Plant Centre; Tudor Restaurant. DISABLED: Limited access in house; Riverside walk & Gardens, Restaurant & Shop all suitable for wheelchairs.

OPENING TIMES: House: 16TH MARCH - 30TH APRIL: 12 noon - 5.00 p.m. (Saturday, Sunday); EASTER MONDAY - WEDNESDAY: 12 noon - 5.00 p.m. (closed Good Friday); MAY -SEPTEMBER: 12 noon - 5.00 p.m. (daily, except Thursday & Friday); OCTOBER 5TH-20TH: 12 noon - 5.00 p.m. (Saturday & Sunday). Last admissions 4.30 p.m. House may close at 4.00 p.m. on Saturday. National Trust members: free admission with membership passes during normal opening hours. Grounds & Restaurant: 11.00 a.m. - 5.30 p.m. on days house is open. Gift Shop & Plant Centre: 11.30 a.m. - 5.30 p.m. on days house is open.

EASTNOR CASTLE, LEDBURY, HEREFORDSHIRE, HR8 1RL.
(01531) - 633160.   Mr & The Hon. Mrs Hervey-Bathurst

Map A; #4. Eastnor Castle is 2½m E of Ledbury on the A438 Tewkesbury road. Alternatively, leave the M50 at Junction 2 towards Ledbury and then take the A449/A438 to Eastnor. Early 19th C Castle in Norman Revival style; Gothic Revival interior by Pugin; Extensive Grounds; Arboretum & Deer Park; Adventure Playground; Children's Maze; Garden Centre; 'Estate Life' Exhibition; Special Events throughout the year; Gift Shop; Tea Room. DISABLED: Disabled and elderly visitors may alight at the Castle entrance. Priority for nearby parking.

OPENING TIMES: EASTER - END OF SEPTEMBER: Sundays & Bank Holiday Mondays: 11.00 a.m. - 5.00 p.m. (last admissions 4.00 p.m.); Every day except Saturdays in JULY & AUGUST: 11.00 a.m. - 5.00 p.m. (last admissions 4.00 p.m.) Parties at other times by appointment.

KELMSCOTT MANOR, KELMSCOTT, NR. LECHLADE, OXON. GL7 3HJ.
(01367) - 252486.   The Society of Antiquaries

Map B: #11. Kelmscott village is 2½m E of Lechlade, signposted from the A417 about 1m E of Lechlade; from the A361 about 1m N of Lechlade. Elizabethan and late 17th C manor house; the country home of William Morris ~ poet, craftsman & socialist ~from 1871 until his death in 1896; Collection of possessions and artefacts of Morris and his associates; Gift Shop; Refreshments in the Stable Barn. DISABLED: Access to the Manor for the disabled is limited; please telephone for further information.

OPENING TIMES: EARLY APRIL ~ LATE SEPTEMBER: 11.00 a.m. - 1.00 p.m. & 2.00 p.m. - 5.00 p.m. (Wednesdays), last admissions 12.30 p.m. & 4.30 p.m. ALSO: the third Saturday each month, April to September: 2.00 p.m. - 5.00 p.m. Last admissions 4.30 p.m. Pre-booked group visits can be arranged on Thursdays & Fridays, April-September.

OWLPEN MANOR, OWLPEN, nr ULEY, GLOUCESTERSHIRE, GL11 5BZ.
(01453) - 860261. Nicholas & Karin Mander

Map B: #12. Owlpen is set in a valley ½m E of Uley, off the B4066. From the M5 take Exits 13 or 14 and head for the B4066. Owlpen is signposted from the centre of Uley. Medieval manor house dating from 1450 to 1616 with minor 18th C improvements and Arts & Crafts restoration in 1926; Formal Gardens; extensive grounds that include the Grist Mill (1728), Court House (1620s) and Victorian Church; Licensed Restaurant. Accommodation available in nine period cottages. DISABLED: The Manor House is unsuitable for wheelchairs.

OPENING TIMES: 1ST APRIL-31ST OCTOBER: 2.00 p.m. - 5.00 p.m. (Tuesday~Sunday & Bank Holiday Mondays. Restaurant open at 12.00 noon. Groups of 30 or more at other times by appointment. Notice of large groups & coaches essential (special rates).

RAGLEY HALL, ALCESTER, WARWICKSHIRE, B49 5NJ.
(01789) - 762090.   The Earl of Yarmouth

Map A; #5. Ragley Hall is 2m SW of Alcester, off the A435/A46, 8m W of Stratford on Avon. Late 17th C Mansion with 18th C additions; 400 acres of parkland; Adventure Wood; Woodland Walk; Rose Gardens; Maze; Carriage Collection; Special Events throughout the year; Bodgers Cabin (light refreshments); licensed Terrace Tea Rooms. DISABLED: Wheelchair ramp to ground floor & toilets; lift to first floor; access to gardens limited.

OPENING TIMES: APRIL - EARLY OCTOBER: 10.00 a.m. - 6.00 p.m. (closed Friday & Monday, except Bank Holiday Mondays). Park open every day in July & August.

STANWAY HOUSE, STANWAY, CHELTENHAM, GLOUCESTERSHIRE, GL54 5PQ.
(01386) - 673469. Lord Neidpath

Map A: #6. Stanway House is just north of the B4077 from Stow-on-the-Wold to Toddington, about 11m W of Stow. Jacobean Mansion; 14th C Tithe Barn; 18th C Pyramid; Extensive Gardens & Grounds; Water Mill; Ice House; Brewery. Refreshments available at Old Bakehouse in village. DISABLED: Limited access.

OPENING TIMES: JUNE - SEPTEMBER: 2.00 p.m. - 5.00 p.m. (Tuesday & Thursday). Other times by appointment only. Guided tours can be arranged for up to 70 people. Stanway also offers function facilities.

STONOR, HENLEY-ON-THAMES, OXFORDSHIRE, RG9 6HF.
(01491) - 638587.   Lord Camoys

Map B: #13. Stonor is on the B480 about 5m N of Henley-on-Thames. Medieval mansion extended in 16th & 18th centuries; Medieval Catholic Chapel; Sanctuary for St. Edmund Campion in 1581; Hillside Gardens; Special Events throughout the summer; Souvenir Gift Shop; Tea Room. DISABLED: Gardens, Shop & Tea Room accessible; wheelchair users please phone in advance.

OPENING TIMES: EARLY APRIL - LATE SEPTEMBER: 2.00 p.m. - 5.30 p.m. (Sundays & Bank Holiday Mondays); also, during the same hours: Wednesdays, MAY - LATE SEPTEMBER; Thursdays, EARLY JULY - LATE AUGUST; Saturdays, EARLY AUGUST. Last admissions, 5.00 p.m. Parties also at other times by appointment, minimum 20 persons.

SUDELEY CASTLE, WINCHCOMBE, GLOUCESTERSHIRE, GL54 5JD.
(01242) - 604357.   Lady Ashcombe

Map A: #7. Sudeley Castle is just south of the B4632 (A46) Cheltenham to Stratford road, about 6m NW of Cheltenham. 15th C Castle, partly restored in the 19th C; Extensive Gardens; Castle Church with tomb of Queen Katherine Parr; Exhibitions on Lace, Emma Dent & The English Table; Wildfowl Sanctuary, with Sudeley's White Peacock; Fort Sudeley Adventure Playground; Castle Gift Shop & Plant Centre; Special Events throughout the year; Restaurant/Tea Rooms. DISABLED: The Castle apartments are not suitable for the disabled, and the gardens have limited access.

OPENING TIMES: MARCH: Gardens, Plant Centre & Shop: 11.00 a.m. - 4.30 p.m. (daily); APRIL-OCTOBER: Gardens, Grounds, Exhibition Centre, Shop, Plant Centre, Restaurant/ Tea Rooms: 10.30 a.m. - 5.30 p.m. (daily); Church: 10.30 a.m. - 5.00 p.m. (daily); Castle Apartments: 11.00 a.m. - 5.00 p.m. (daily).

WHITTINGTON COURT, WHITTINGTON, CHELTENHAM, GL54 4HF.
(01242) - 820556.   Mr & Mrs Jack Stringer

Map B: #14. Whittington Court is in the village of Whittington, just off the A40, 4m E of Cheltenham. Cotswold manor house of 16th & 17th C.; 13th C Church; 17th C Barn. DISABLED: Access to ground floor of Court & Church.

OPENING TIMES: EACH YEAR: EASTER SATURDAY and the following 15 days AND 17 days before, and including the AUGUST BANK HOLIDAY: 2.00 p.m. - 5.00 p.m. (daily).

Tourist Information Centres

Each of these Information Centres is close to at least one of the houses featured in this book. Except for those marked with an asterisk they are open all year round.

BANBURY
Banbury Museum
8, Horsefair
Oxfordshire
OX16 0AA
(01295) - 259855

*BROADWAY
1 Cotswold Court
Worcestershire
WR12 7AA
(01386) - 852937

CHELTENHAM
77 Promenade
Gloucestershire
GL50 1PP
(01242) - 522878

EVESHAM
The Almonry
Abbey Gate
Worcestershire
WR11 4BG
(01386) - 446944

* FARINGDON
The Pump House
5 Market Place
Oxfordshire
SN7 7HL
(01367) - 242191

GLOUCESTER
St Michael's Tower
The Cross
Gloucestershire
GL1 1PD
(01452) - 421188

HENLEY ON THAMES
Town Hall
Market Place
Oxfordshire
RG9 2AQ
(01491) - 578034

LEDBURY
1 Church Lane
Herefordshire
HR8 1DH
(01531) - 636147

NUNEATON
Nuneaton Library
Church Street Warwickshire
CV11 4DR
(01203) - 384027

OXFORD
The Old School
Gloucester Green
Oxfordshire
OX1 2DA
(01865) - 726871

STRATFORD UPON AVON
Bridgefoot
Warwickshire
CV37 6GW
(01789) - 293127

STROUD
Subscription Rooms
George Street
Gloucestershire
GL5 1AE
(01453) - 765768

* TETBURY
The Old Court House
63 Long Street
Gloucestershire
GL8 8AA
(01666) - 503552

WALLINGFORD
Town Hall
Market Place
Oxfordshire
OX10 0EG
(01491) - 826972

*WINCHCOMBE
Town Hall
High Street
Gloucestershire
GL54 5LJ
(01242) - 602925

WOODSTOCK
Hensington Road
Oxfordshire
OX20 1JQ
(01993) - 811038